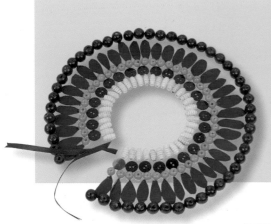

THE ANCIENT EGYPTIANS

DRESS, EAT, WRITE AND PLAY JUST LIKE THE EGYPTIANS

FIONA MACDONALD

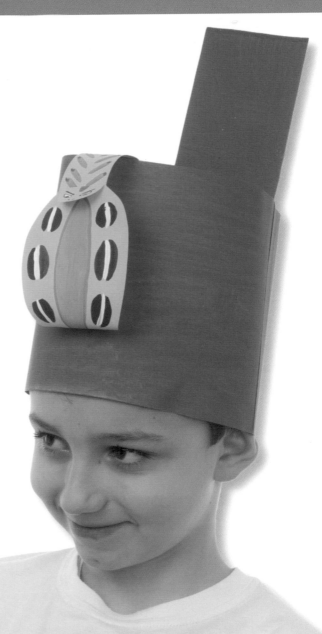

QED Publishing

First published in the UK in 2007 by
QED Publishing
A Quarto Group company
226 City Road
London EC1V 2TT
www.qed-publishing.co.uk

A catalogue record for this book is available from the British
Library.

ISBN 978 1 84538 653 5

Written by Fiona Macdonald
Editor Felicity Fitchard
Designer Liz Wiffen
Projects made by Veronica Erard

Publisher Steve Evans
Creative Director Zeta Davies
Senior Editor Hannah Ray

Printed and bound in China

Picture credits

Key: t = top, b = bottom, c = centre, l = left, r = right,
fc = front cover

The Art Archive: p4 br: Luxor Museum, Egypt/Dagli Orti; p6
bl, p8 tl, p14 tr, p24 tl, p26 bl: Dagli Orti; p8 br, p28 bl: Musée du
Louvre Paris/Dagli Orti; p12 br: Egyptian Museum Turin/Dagli
Orti; p16 ct: Bibliotheque des Arts Décoratifs Paris/Dagli Orti;
p16 bl: Pharaonic Village Cairo/Dagli Orti; p18 tl, p20 bl:
Egyptian Museum Cairo/Dagli Orti.

Corbis: p12 tl: Burnstein Collection; p22 bl, p28 tl: Sandro Vannini.

Werner Forman Archive: p4 tl, p6 tr, p10 tr, p10 bl: Egyptian
Museum Cairo; p14 bl: E. Strouhal; p18 bl.

Words in **bold** are explained
in the glossary on page 30.

CONTENTS

WHO WERE THE ANCIENT EGYPTIANS?

The Egyptians lived beside the River Nile in Egypt, North Africa. They were originally **nomads** who discovered that the rich soil along the banks of the Nile made it a good place to find and grow food. About 8000 years ago, they **settled** on the east side of the Nile. They built villages, grew crops and kept animals. Their leaders created new kingdoms in Upper (south) and Lower (north) Egypt.

Pharaoh Tutankhamun is famous for the treasures found in his tomb.

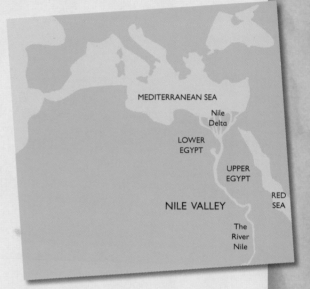

MEDITERRANEAN SEA

Nile Delta

LOWER EGYPT

UPPER EGYPT

RED SEA

NILE VALLEY

The River Nile

This map shows the Nile Valley in Egypt.

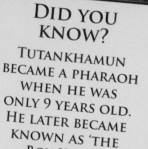

DID YOU KNOW?
TUTANKHAMUN BECAME A PHARAOH WHEN HE WAS ONLY 9 YEARS OLD. HE LATER BECAME KNOWN AS 'THE BOY KING'.

ONE KINGDOM
Around 3100 BCE the two kingdoms joined together under one king, called the **pharaoh**. The Egyptians believed he was the son of their Sun-god, Amun-Re. The new kingdom became rich and powerful. It grew into a civilization that lasted for the next 3000 years.

A GREAT CIVILIZATION
Most Egyptians were farmers, traders or craftworkers. However there were also many educated and highly skilled men including scientists, **scribes** and priests. Together, the Egyptians created a strong, well-organized society. From massive pyramids to beautiful jewellery, many things that they created have survived for us to admire today.

When northern and southern Egypt become one kingdom, pharaohs wore a double crown called a pschent (say pz-shent).

4

MAKE A PHARAOH'S CROWN

A cobra, symbol of the snake-goddess Wadjet, decorated each pharaoh's crown. It was meant to protect him, and his kingdom, from harm.

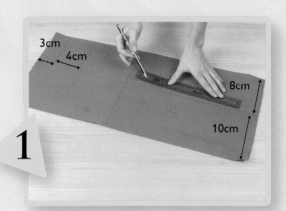

1

From red card, cut a rectangle that's long enough to go round your head and 18cm wide. Add lines as shown.

2

Cut out the shape. Fix double-sided sticky tape to one short end. Roll up into a cylinder. Press in place.

3

Draw a snake-headed strip on the yellow card. Cut it out. Use felt-tip pens or paint to decorate both sides.

4

Fix the end of the snake inside the crown. Make a loop and fix the snake's body to the outside.

5

Curl the snake's body back up and fix it to itself using a strip of double-sided sticky tape.

Pharaohs wore a red crown, like this, to show they ruled Lower Egypt. They added a white one to make a pschent. ▶

5

THE MIGHTY NILE

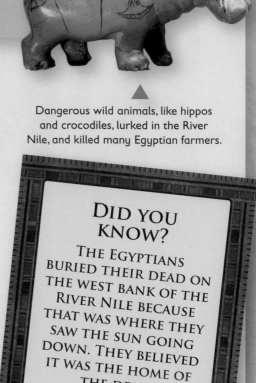

ost of Egypt was hot, dry desert. Egyptians called this deshret (Red Land). Little could live there, apart from a few tough, wild animals. The River Nile flowed through the vast desert, from south to north, bringing life-giving water to the Egyptians. The river provided drinking water and water for their animals and crops. They washed in the Nile, fished in it and used it as a water-highway to transport people and goods. The Egyptians even made boats from the **papyrus** reeds that grew along its banks.

Dangerous wild animals, like hippos and crocodiles, lurked in the River Nile, and killed many Egyptian farmers.

DID YOU KNOW?

THE EGYPTIANS BURIED THEIR DEAD ON THE WEST BANK OF THE RIVER NILE BECAUSE THAT WAS WHERE THEY SAW THE SUN GOING DOWN. THEY BELIEVED IT WAS THE HOME OF THE DEAD.

The man (centre) is holding a throwing stick which hunters used to stun birds.

SUPER SOIL

Once a year, the river burst its banks, flooding the land on either side. This left a layer of thick mud behind, creating a strip of rich, fertile soil on both sides of the river. Egyptians called this **kemet** (Black Land). Crops grew quickly in kemet mud. By digging **irrigation** canals (long ditches) the Egyptians brought river water to their plants during the dry spring months.

RIVER OF LIFE

The Egyptians could not have survived without the Nile – they even used kemet mud to make bricks to build their homes. They built villages above the **flood plains** on the east bank, which they thought was full of life and energy – like the rising sun.

MAKE A REED BOAT

The Egyptians used light boats made from papyrus reeds for short journeys up and down the river. Make your own floating boat!

YOU WILL NEED:
16 BENDY DRINKING STRAWS • NARROW MASKING TAPE • WHITE STRING • WASHING-UP BOWL (OPTIONAL)

1 Pull out the short end of each straw to extend the bendy section. Repeat until all 16 straws are full length.

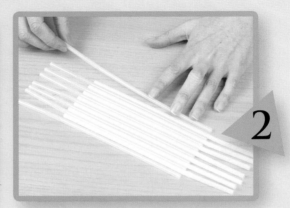

2 Line the straws up with eight pointing one way and eight the other way, alternately.

3 Stick the straws together using masking tape as shown. Make sure there are no gaps between straws.

4 Gather up one set of bendy ends. Wrap string round and tie them all together. Repeat at the other end.

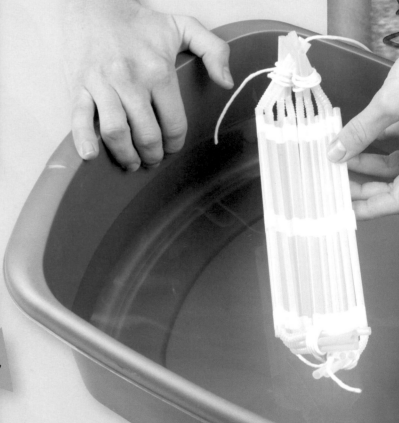

Half-fill a washing-up bowl with water and launch your reed boat. ▶

COWS AND CROPS

An Egyptian farmer using a plough pulled by oxen to prepare his fields for planting crops. His wife walks behind him, scattering seeds on the freshly ploughed earth.

The Egyptians called their rich farmland 'a gift from the gods'. It produced excellent, plentiful crops. Each farmer gave some of their harvest as tax to the pharaoh. Whatever they had left over they might **barter** for goods, such as pottery. Egyptian farmers also raised sheep, cattle and goats. As well as providing milk, meat and leather, cattle also pulled ploughs and carts.

THE YEARLY CYCLE

Every year in the middle of summer, the Nile overflowed and flooded the valley. By autumn, the water ebbed away and farmers planted wheat and barley seeds in the rich soil it left behind. Farmers also grew grape vines, fig trees, melons, beans, lentils, garlic, lettuce and dates. As soon as the crops were ripe, they had to be harvested and stored. Then the irrigation ditches were repaired, before the next flood. When it came, it covered the fields for the next few months.

RIVER RICHES

The Egyptians went fishing in the Nile, and hunted wild birds along its banks. They also harvested papyrus reeds to make paper, sandals and other useful objects. Since there were almost no trees in the desert, most people did not have wooden furniture. Instead, they had mats and baskets made from reeds.

DID YOU KNOW?

EGYPTIAN FARMERS KEPT CATS TO PROTECT THEIR GRAIN-STORES FROM RATS AND MICE. THE EGYPTIAN WORD FOR CAT WAS 'MIW'!

To make papyrus (the first paper) the Egyptians cut thin strips of papyrus reed stalk, soaked them, laid them flat, then pressed them together.

Make Your Own Papyrus Paper

The Egyptians invented paper. They made it from strips of papyrus reed, soaked in water then pressed together. Try making your own!

YOU WILL NEED:
A5 SHEET PALE GREEN PAPER • A5 SHEET DARK GREEN PAPER • SCISSORS • PVA MIXTURE (3 PARTS PVA TO ONE PART WATER) • PLASTIC TRAY • KITCHEN PAPER

1 Draw a 1cm margin along the long edge of the pale paper. Repeat along the short edge of the darker paper.

2 Cut 1cm-wide strips across the pale paper, up to the margin. Cut strips into the dark paper, up to the margin.

3 Weave the two pieces of paper together. Weave each strip over, then under, along the row.

4 Half-fill the plastic tray with PVA mixture. Place your paper completely in the PVA mixture.

5 Pat your paper with kitchen towel to remove excess moisture. Peg to an indoor washing line. Leave to dry.

Impress your friends with your hand-made notepaper. ▶

9

HOME AND FAMILY

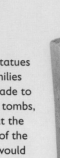

Egyptians were sociable people. Family life was important to them. They also valued peaceful communities and helpful neighbours. Men and women married in their early teens. They liked large families and hoped to have lots of children. Marriages were arranged by the girl's parents. Egyptian husbands could have more than one wife, but wives could only have one husband.

Stone statues of families were made to stand in tombs, so that the spirits of the dead would visit them. ▶

DID YOU KNOW?

MANY CHILDREN DIED FROM INFECTIOUS DISEASES. MOTHERS TRIED TO PROTECT THEM WITH MAGIC SPELLS AND AMULETS (LUCKY CHARMS).

YOU WILL NEED:

THICK CARD 22 x 8cm • PENCIL • RULER • BLACK FELT-TIP PEN • AIR-DRYING CLAY POSTER PAINT AND BRUSHES • DICE

PLAY SENET

All Egyptians, from the pharaoh to farmers, loved to play board games!

Senet was the most popular board game in Egypt. It was played on a board marked in squares, using counters made of bone or ivory.

1

In pencil, draw a 20 x 6cm rectangle on the card. Mark off 2cm intervals along all four sides.

2

Join up your marks to make a grid. Go over the grid and round the outer edge in black felt-tip pen.

LIFE AT HOME

Most Egyptians lived in homes with just one or two rooms and a flat roof. People often cooked and slept on the roof. The homes of the rich were much larger, with ornamental pools and gardens. But rich or poor, all houses were made from mud bricks that had dried solid in the sun.

DAILY TASKS

A typical household might include parents, aunts, uncles, grandparents, cousins, servants and slaves. Women ran the home, cooked the food, made clothes and fetched water. They also cared for old or ill family members. Families ran farms, workshops and market stalls as a team. At the end of the working day, they liked to relax together and might play board games.

HOW TO PLAY
RULES FOR TWO PLAYERS

When the board is set up, take turns to roll the dice and move one counter at a time forward. You can move any of your counters as long as you do not land on a square that already contains one of your own counters. If you land on one of your opponent's counters, send them back to where you were.

The first player to get all their counters off the board wins!

START

Direction of play ▶

FINISH

▲
Before you start, position the counters along the top row, alternating the colours. This board shows a game that has already begun.

3 Roll 10 small balls of clay. Mould each one into cone shape. Make sure the bottom is as flat as possible.

4 Once the clay is hard, paint five cones blue and five yellow. When they're dry, you're ready to play!

EATING AND DRINKING

A kneeling woman servant crushes wheat grains between a stone slab and a stone roller to make coarse, gritty flour.

Egyptians ate one main meal a day, at noon, when it was too hot to be out in the sun. Sometimes, they also had a light snack for breakfast or supper. All the cooking was done by women and servants. The Egyptians had no way of keeping food fresh, so each meal had to be prepared from scratch. It was tough, tiring work. Egyptians ate bread, soup, fish, vegetables and fruit, and drank home-made beer.

BREAD AND BEER

Flour was made by grinding the grain by hand, using a grinding stone. Water was added to make bread dough, which was then kneaded and baked in an oven. Rich people ate white bread and everyone else ate rough, brown bread. Beer was made by mixing bread and water, and leaving it to **ferment**.

DID YOU KNOW?

MOST BREAD CONTAINED TINY PIECES OF GRIT FROM THE GRINDING STONES. THE GRIT WORE PEOPLES' TEETH AWAY.

Male servants kneading dough in a big pot, baking bread in a clay oven, grinding flour, and carrying a tray loaded with loaves and little cakes.

THE HIGH LIFE

Rich people had servants to prepare food for them. They also enjoyed luxuries, such as roast meat, wine and honey cakes. On special occasions, they held feasts with music and dancing.

MAKE FUL MEDAMES

Ful Medames means 'bean stew'. The Egyptians ate many different bean-based meals. Adding an egg to this recipe was a great luxury!

1

Ask an adult to hard boil two eggs. Put the eggs under the cold tap to cool them, then peel off their shells.

2

Put the peeled eggs in a mixing bowl and use a fork to mash them up into small pieces. Now drain the beans.

3

Put the eggs in a saucepan and add the mixed beans. Crush the garlic in the garlic press, over the pan.

4

Add a tablespoon of olive oil and mix everything together thoroughly. Serve with lettuce and bread.

Arrange the lettuce in a circle to hold the bean stew like a leafy bowl. ▶

13

LOOKING GOOD

The Egyptians cared a lot about their appearance. They liked to look clean, young, slim and healthy. They made face cream from animal fat and plant oils, and perfume from plant gum. Men and women both wore heavy green or grey eyeliner made from **minerals**. The Egyptians believed this protected their eyes from harm. Most clothes were made of linen. Women and older girls wore long robes. Men and boys wore knee-length kilts.

HAIR STYLES

Rich men and women shaved their heads and wore wigs. Fashions changed over time, from long and flowing wigs to short braids and curls. Ordinary people kept their own natural hair. Boys' heads were shaved or partly shaved, except for a ponytail on one side called 'the lock of youth'.

FASHIONS

The basic design of ordinary people's clothes stayed the same for centuries. Pharaohs, queens and nobles experimented with fashionable styles. All Egyptians, rich or poor, wore bracelets, necklaces and charms called amulets. The rich wore enormous jewelled collars made from gold, glass and **semi-precious** stones. Poorer people made their collars from clay beads.

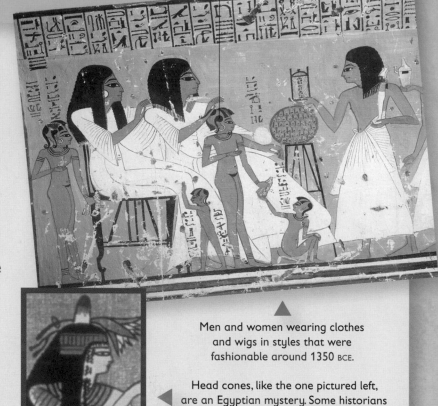

Lock of youth

▲ Men and women wearing clothes and wigs in styles that were fashionable around 1350 BCE.

◄ Head cones, like the one pictured left, are an Egyptian mystery. Some historians believe that they were made of perfumed wax that released scent as it melted.

DID YOU KNOW?

MANY EGYPTIAN CHILDREN WORE NO CLOTHES AT ALL UNTIL THEY WERE OLD ENOUGH TO MARRY, AT AROUND 12 YEARS OLD. SOME SERVANTS ALSO WENT NAKED.

◄ Queen Nefertari, dressed in a tight, patterned robe, fashionable around 1500 BCE. She also wears thick eyeliner, a heavy jewelled collar and bracelets on both arms.

14

MAKE AN EGYPTIAN COLLAR

Neck collars were made from semi-precious stones or gold, clay or glass beads. How many pretty bits and pieces can you find for yours?

YOU WILL NEED:
SQUARE OF FELT 40 x 40 cm
• PAIR OF COMPASSES
• SCISSORS • GLUE • GEMS,
BUTTONS, SEQUINS, FELT
SCRAPS • RED RIBBON

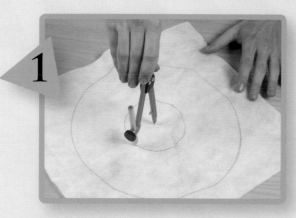

1

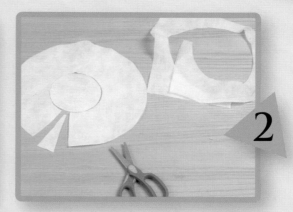

2

Set your compass to 12cm and draw a circle. Now set it to 4cm and draw another from the same point.

Cut both circles out. Then cut away a small section of the collar shape, as shown here.

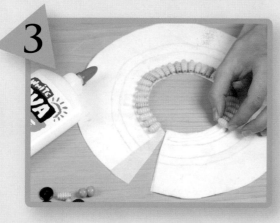

3

4

Put a line of glue around the inside of the collar and place different coloured beads along it.

Add another line of glue and more buttons. In this way, continue to build up the pattern.

5

On each side of the collar, glue one end of a length of red ribbon to the felt backing.

Put your collar on and tie at the back. For a real Egyptian look, you could add a headband!

DESIGN AND TECHNOLOGY

Craftsmen at work. They are melting gold (top left), shaping vases (top right), polishing a huge jar (bottom left) and carving decorations (bottom middle).

The Egyptians were brilliant problem-solvers. They invented a calendar, built enormous pyramids and created one of the world's first ways of writing. Most Egyptians couldn't read or write, but some educated people studied mathematics, medicine, **astronomy** and engineering.

MAKE A WATER-CLOCK

Measure time the Egyptian way, by watching water-levels change inside your clock. You need a friend or a volunteer from the family to help!

YOU WILL NEED:
LARGE YOGHURT POT • RULER • WATERPROOF MARKER PEN • OLD NEWSPAPER • PVA MIXTURE (3 PARTS PVA TO ONE PART WATER) • PAINTS AND BRUSHES • JUG • WATCH • FRIEND

1

Using a ruler and a marker pen, mark off 5mm intervals on the inside of the pot.

The water always drips through at the same speed, so you can see how much time has passed by looking at the markings inside.

4

Hold the pot over a sink with your finger over the hole. Ask your friend to pour water up to the top mark.

16

ARTISTIC ARTISANS

Craftsmen, including metalsmiths, glassworkers and potters, were well respected. With simple tools they produced stunning objects. The best craftworkers were employed by the pharaoh to build palaces, temples and tombs. They were paid in grain, fish, salt and sometimes wine. Other craftworkers lived in busy manufacturing districts in towns or larger villages. They sold their goods by bartering them at markets or at their workshops.

TRADE AND TREASURES

Gold, semi-precious stones, ivory from elephant tusks and ebony from tropical trees were all **imported**. The Egyptians were great traders and made adventurous journeys to bring back treasures from distant lands.

2

Cover the outside of the pot with newspaper strips dipped into PVA mixture. Leave to dry completely.

3

Ask an adult to make a small hole in the bottom of the pot. Paint the pot and add Egyptian-style decorations.

5

Is your friend ready to time this bit? Remove your finger. When the water level reaches the next mark, say 'stop!'

Keep timing how long it takes the water level to go down from one mark to the next. What do you notice?

17

MIGHTY PHARAOHS

This is the coffin of Tutankhamun. He is holding a shepherd's crook to show that a pharaoh guards his people just as a shepherd guards his sheep.

Every Egyptian had to be loyal and obedient to the pharaoh. The Egyptians believed the pharaoh was a living link between people and the gods. When a pharaoh died, he himself became a god. Each pharaoh had many duties. He was chief priest, army commander and national leader. He planned government policy and made new laws. A pharaoh also had to protect Egypt's frontiers, encourage trade and conquer new land.

FAMOUS PHARAOHS

Pharaohs were almost always men. The names of the greatest are still remembered today: Rameses II defeated invaders; Akhenaten built a new capital and founded a new religion; Tutankhamun was buried in a treasure-filled tomb. But a few extraordinary women also ruled Egypt. The most famous is Hatshepsut (say Hat-shep-soot), who took over power from her stepson. She paid for magnificent buildings and sent ships to explore the east coast of Africa.

DID YOU KNOW?

TO SHOW HIS SPECIAL STATUS, THE PHARAOH WORE A FALSE BEARD. IT WAS A SIGN OF STRENGTH.

Pharaohs paid for huge portraits of themselves. This pharaoh is standing between two goddesses.

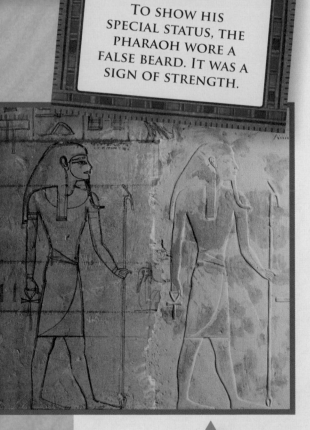

These stone carvings were never finished so you can still see the artist's markings on the left.

PAINT YOURSELF A PHARAOH

Pose as a pharaoh and paint an impressive, life-size portrait for your bedroom wall. You will need some help from a friend!

YOU WILL NEED:
ROLL OF BROWN PAPER • MEASURING TAPE • SCISSORS • MASKING TAPE • PENCIL • PAINT AND BRUSHES • BLACK FELT-TIP PEN • FRIEND • ADHESIVE PUTTY

1 Measure your own height. Add 30cm to your height and cut off a piece of brown paper that length.

2 Put the paper on the floor and use a piece of masking tape to hold down each of the corners.

3 Lie down on the paper in your chosen Egyptian pose. Ask your friend to draw round you in pencil.

When dry, carefully go over the details with black felt-tip pen. Now put your figure up on the wall with adhesive putty.

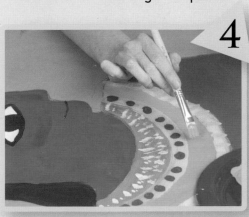

4 Draw on patterns and a face with an Egyptian eye. Paint your portrait, using lots of bright colours.

SKILFUL SCRIBES

Only four Egyptians out of every thousand could read and write. Scribes earned their living by writing. Many scribes had important jobs in government. The pharaoh needed them to keep written records of royal and government business, such as new laws and huge building projects. Training to be a scribe started young, when boys were sent to schools at royal temples.

Hieroglyphs were used to write religious or magic words. This is a page of magic spells, to help dead people in the Afterlife (see page 28). ▶

SCHOOL LIFE

At school, trainee scribes learned to read and write hieroglyphs – Egyptian picture-writing. A scribe needed to know at least 700 of these picture signs. They copied out and recited hieroglyph scripts to practise their reading and writing skills.

DID YOU KNOW?
SCRIBES USED A REED PEN AND BLACK INK, MADE FROM SOOT. THEY USED RED INK FOR IMPORTANT WORDS.

HIEROGLYPHS

Each hieroglyph can stand for an object or a sound, and what it means depends on the other pictures it is with. The picture signs can be read in three different directions: right to left, left to right or top to bottom. Royal names were always pictured inside a rope loop called a cartouche (say kar-toosh).

A portrait of an Egyptian pharaoh or queen often included their name written in hieroglyphs. Once historians realized this, ◀ they were able to match hieroglyphs to the alphabet and gradually break the code of the hieroglyphs.

MAKE A NAME PLAQUE

Choose an Egyptian name for yourself and write it in hieroglyphs. Surround it with a cartouche, like a queen or pharaoh.

1

Paint the card pale brown. When dry, draw on a 10 x 3cm rectangle with rounded corners. Cut it out.

BOYS   **GIRLS**

Nebtawi   Wosent

Rawer   Nitokris

Papkapu   Cleopatra

2

Choose a name for yourself and carefully copy the hieroglyphs onto your rectangle in pencil.

3

With felt-tip pens, go over your new name. Then put a thin line of glue around the edge of the card.

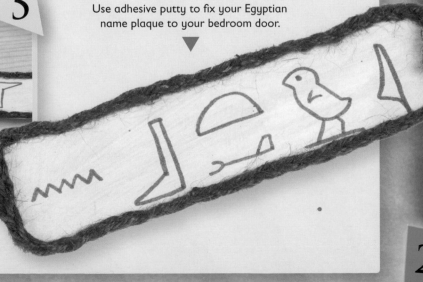

4

Take hold of the wool 5 or 6cm down from the end. From this point, press it onto the glue. Do a little at a time.

Use adhesive putty to fix your Egyptian name plaque to your bedroom door.

▼

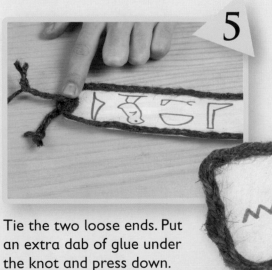

5

Tie the two loose ends. Put an extra dab of glue under the knot and press down.

21

GODS AND MAGIC

The Egyptians thought that gods and goddesses made the world and controlled everything that happened within it. They worshipped hundreds of different gods. Some were local gods, connected to one village, town or temple. The Egyptians believed in magic and charms, that dreams had meanings, and in life after death.

Anubis (say An-ew-biss) was the god of death. He had the head of a fierce wild dog called a jackal. ▶

The mightiest gods, such as Horus, lord of the sky, were worshipped throughout Egypt. The eye of Horus was a healing charm.

▼

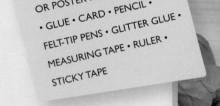

YOU WILL NEED:
AIR-DRYING CLAY • ACRYLIC OR POSTER PAINT • BRUSHES • GLUE • CARD • PENCIL • FELT-TIP PENS • GLITTER GLUE • MEASURING TAPE • RULER • STICKY TAPE

MAKE A SCARAB ARMBAND

The scarab beetle was one of the most popular designs for lucky amulets and jewellery. Make a stunning armband in a few, simple steps.

Scarab beetles were linked to the sun, life and birth. ▶ The Egyptians believed that the small balls of dung that scarab beetles rolled along represented the sun crossing the sky.

1

Warm the clay up in your hands and then make the shape of the scarab beetle, roughly 2.5cm long.

4

Paint the main areas. Leave to dry. Then add details with a fine brush or pens. Lastly, add glitter glue.

22

GODS AND GODDESSES

Egyptian gods and goddesses were shown in many different forms. Some looked like humans, some looked like animals. Each ruled over a special part of life. For example, Nut was the sky goddess, Osiris (say Oz-eye-riss) was god of life after death, Thoth was the god of writing and Hathor (say Hay-thor) was the goddess of music and love. Amun-Re (say Ah-mun-ray), the sun-god, was the most powerful of all.

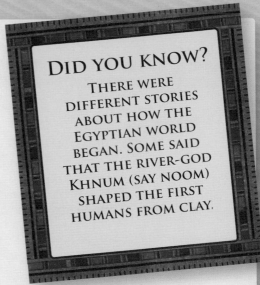

SHRINES

Egyptian people built small shrines inside their own homes. These were dedicated to household and family gods, such as lion-headed Bes, or Tawaret, the hippopotamus goddess. Both protected mothers and children from harm. The Egyptians also wore amulets, chanted spells and visited fortune-tellers.

2

Once the clay has dried out, mix up turquoise paint and paint the scarab. Leave to dry, then add details.

3

Glue the scarab to a piece of card and, in pencil, draw the sun above its head and wings on both sides.

5

Cut out a 3cm-wide card strip to go round your arm with an overlap Cut out your scarab and glue to the card.

Wrap your armband around your arm and tape in place.

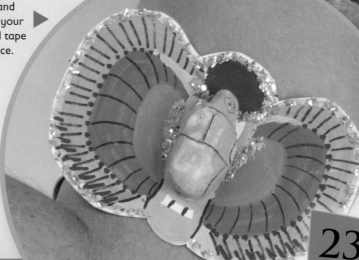

23

TREMENDOUS TEMPLES

Pharaohs built temples as homes for gods and goddesses. Each one housed a holy statue, which was cared for by priests as if it were alive. They washed it, clothed it, said prayers to it, burned **incense** for it and left it gifts, food and drink every day. Temple dancers and musicians performed to please it and young women from noble families were offered to it as wives.

These carvings on a massive temple gateway are over 2300 years old. Originally, they were painted, but the colours have worn away.

DID YOU KNOW?
TEMPLES WERE DECORATED WITH STATUES AND CARVINGS DISPLAYING THE PHARAOH'S NAME AND ACHIEVEMENTS.

TEMPLES
Temples were some of the most magnificent buildings in Egypt. Huge gateways and vast courtyards, with statues and pillars, guarded the entrance to a private, sacred shrine. Only priests could go inside. Royal temples were also used by pharaohs as centres of local government.

Well-trained dancers and musicians performed three times each day while gifts were being offered to the gods.

HOLY ANIMALS
Some temples were homes to holy animals that the Egyptians thought were the living images of their gods. For example, cats represented Bast, the goddess of healing. The spirit of Bast watched over the Temple at Bubastis and many **mummified** cats were buried there. At festivals, holy animals were led through crowds of worshippers waiting to be blessed.

Make a Ceremonial Sistrum

Women dancers shook rattles called sistrums each time gifts were offered to the gods at the temple. Follow the steps to make your own!

YOU WILL NEED:
A4 PIECE CORRUGATED CARD • PENCIL • CRAFT KNIFE • YELLOW PAINT AND BRUSH • RULER • 3 x 25cm LENGTHS OF STRING • STICKY TAPE • 6 TOY BELLS

1

Draw the sistrum shape so that it fills your A4 card. Ask an adult to cut it out. Paint it yellow. Leave to dry.

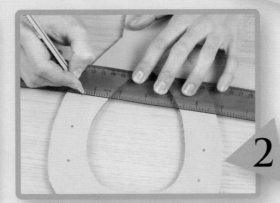

2

Use a ruler to make 3 pairs of parallel marks on each side. Ask an adult to make holes on your marks.

3

Feed string through a top hole and knot. Tape end to back. About 2cm along the string, add a bell and knot.

4

Add another bell. Feed the end of the string through the parallel hole. Pull the string taut and tape to back.

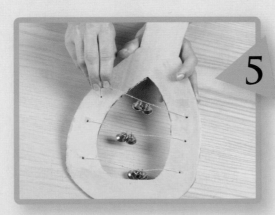

5

Repeat steps 3 and 4 to add two more strings with bells. Then wrap gold ribbon around the handle.

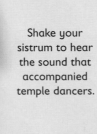

Shake your sistrum to hear the sound that accompanied temple dancers.

PYRAMIDS AND TOMBS

Three of the greatest Egyptian pyramids, at Giza. Originally, they were covered with slabs of white limestone, and tipped with real gold.

Egyptians made some of the world's most spectacular tombs. Tombs were **memorials**, reminding everyone of a dead pharaoh's powers. Just as importantly, they protected and preserved the body buried inside. Tombs were built by gangs of ordinary farmers, as a way of paying tax that they owed the pharaoh. Expert craftsmen added decorations, such as paintings and carvings.

These tomb wall paintings show the kingdom of Osiris, the Egyptian god who helped the dead carry on living in the Afterlife.

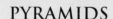

PYRAMIDS

The first Egyptian graves were marked with piles of stones. These were later replaced by brick boxes. The first pyramid-shaped tomb was built around 2650 BCE. For the next 500 years, pharaohs were buried in massive pyramids. The Great Pyramid at Giza is one of the biggest stone buildings ever constructed.

ROCK TOMBS

Eventually, the Egyptians stopped building pyramids and instead cut deep chambers into rocky cliffs. Inside, these rock tombs were decorated with peaceful scenes of family life showing what the Egyptians hoped the Afterlife might be like.

26

MAKE A PYRAMID

Make a gleaming, white pyramid from card. Once you've finished, you can hide your own treasures deep inside the pyramid.

YOU WILL NEED:
SPARE CARD • RULER • PENCIL • CRAFT KNIFE • A3 SHEET OF WHITE CARD • SCISSORS • DOUBLE-SIDED STICKY TAPE • GOLD PAINT AND BRUSH OR GOLD PEN

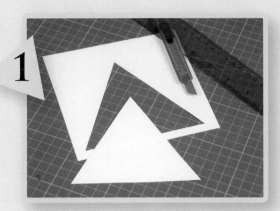

1 Draw a triangle with 12cm sides on spare card. Ask an adult to cut it out with a craft knife and ruler.

2 Place it on a big sheet of card and draw round it. Line it up beside the outline and draw round it again.

3 Draw two more triangles using the same method. Now draw on a 5mm-wide tab as shown.

4 Cut around the outer edge of your shape. Ask an adult to score along all the inner lines.

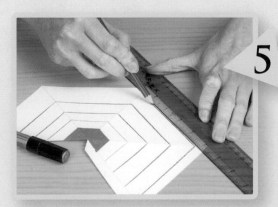

5 Colour the tip of the pyramid gold using paint or gold pen. Add lines to show the limestone panels.

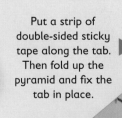
Put a strip of double-sided sticky tape along the tab. Then fold up the pyramid and fix the tab in place. ▶

AMAZING MUMMIES

The Egyptians believed that the spirit of a dead person would live on for ever in the Afterlife, as long as their body did not rot away. **Embalming** was a technique the Egyptians developed to preserve dead bodies. The first mummies were made by chance when dead bodies dried out in Egypt's hot climate and were naturally preserved by salts in the desert sand. Over time, the Egyptians developed more elaborate ways of making mummies.

◀ The bandage-wrapped mummy was placed inside a wooden coffin that was decorated inside and out, often with gold leaf.

YOU WILL NEED:
AIR-DRYING CLAY •
MODELLING TOOL •
ACRYLIC PAINT AND
BRUSHES • MARKER PENS

MAKE A SHABTI SERVANT

Shape a shabti servant from clay. You could make several, each with different hair and patterns on their body.

Two female shabtis stand outside a fine decorated box, made for them to 'live' in while they waited inside a tomb.

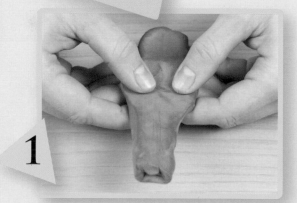

1

Warm the clay up in your hands. Then mould the shape of the figure. Don't forget her upturned feet.

3

Mix up stone-coloured paint. Paint your figure all over, except her face and hands. Leave to dry.

MAKING A MUMMY

First, the dead body was cut open, then the soft inner organs were removed and the space was filled with desert salt. After 70 days, the body was padded with cloth to look lifelike, and wrapped in linen bandages soaked in plant gum. Magic amulets were tucked in between each layer of bandages. Then the mummy was placed in a beautifully decorated coffin.

READY FOR THE AFTERLIFE

Food, clothes, games and anything else a person might need in the Afterlife were placed in the tomb, close to the coffin. Small figures called shabtis were also included. These were models of servants who would do any work the gods demanded, leaving the dead person's spirit free and at peace.

> ### DID YOU KNOW?
>
> THE EGYPTIANS MUMMIFIED ANIMALS, TOO, INCLUDING CATS, BIRDS, DOGS AND EVEN WHOLE BULLS!

2 Roll out two sausages for her arms. Cross them over at the front. Use a modelling tool to draw on her face.

4 Paint her hair blue. Then use marker pens to draw on her face, collar and the hieroglyphs on her body.

Now your shabti is complete. Be like the Egyptians, and use left-over clay to make little model farm tools, cooking pots and baskets for her.

GLOSSARY

amulet Lucky charm, usually small and worn as jewellery.

astronomy The study of the Sun, Moon, stars and planets.

barter Exchange goods for others of equal value.

embalming Preserving a corpse (dead body) so that it does not rot. The Egyptians used salt, oils, spices and plant gum.

ferment When yeasts (tiny plants) feed on sugar in a mixture they give off gas and it becomes frothy or bubbly.

flood plains Flat areas of land bordering a river that get flooded regularly.

imported Goods that are brought into a country from foreign lands.

incense Mixture of herbs and spices which gives off sweet-smelling smoke when burnt.

irrigation Bringing water to dry land, using ditches or canals, so that crops will grow.

kemet Fertile mud left behind by the River Nile floods.

memorials Statues, inscriptions or carvings designed to help people remember the dead.

minerals Natural rocks, metals and salts.

mummified A corpse (dead body) that has been embalmed (see above) and then wrapped in bandages before being buried.

nomad Person who regularly moves from place to place, to hunt wild animals and gather wild food.

papyrus Papyrus reeds grew beside the River Nile. Paper made from the stalks of the reeds was called papyrus.

pharaoh King. The name comes from two Egyptian words *per* meaning 'great' or 'royal' and *ah* meaning 'house' or 'palace'.

scribe Trained man or woman who reads and writes to earn a living.

semi-precious Jewel-like stones that are valuable but not as rare as precious stones.

settled When people live in one place all year round.

• In the past, many mummies were destroyed by the people investigating them, but the children can use the latest computer technology to find out what's inside a mummy – without unwrapping it or harming it at all. Go to http://www.thebritishmuseum.ac.uk/childrenscompass/ and follow links to children's compass. Click on 'Tours' and then 'Journey into the Mummy'.

• Egyptian men and women all liked to look good. Research ancient Egyptian make-up, skin care, wigs and hairstyles at the library or on the internet. (See http://www.mnsu.edu/emuseum/prehistory/egypt/dailylife/beautyaids.html and http://www.mnsu.edu/emuseum/prehistory/egypt/dailylife/hairstyles.html). Collect together some modern cosmetics and help the children make themselves up as Egyptians. Have a gentle cleanser at the ready!

• Children can go to http://hieroglyphs.net/000501/html/000-042.html and see their name translated into hieroglyphs. This site also contains interesting information about Ancient Egyptian language and writing. For further research, try http://www.pbs.org/wgbh/nova/pyramid/hieroglyph/.

• Research the original description of the discovery of Tutankhamun's tomb at the library or on the internet (see http://www.nationalgeographic.com/egypt/ or http://www.ashmolean.org/gri/4tut.html). Describe the event to the children and ask them to write an imaginary entry in Howard Carter's diary on the day the treasure was revealed. The children can explore Tutankhamun's tomb online at http://www.kingtutone.com/tutankhamun/enter/.

• Organize an Egyptian gods and goddesses fancy dress party. For costume and other information visit http://www.metmuseum.org/explore/newegypt/htm/th_frame.htm. Click 'Ancient Egyptian Beliefs' then 'Gods and Goddesses'. Help the children to write labels describing the powers and qualities of the deity they are dressed as to pin on their costumes.

• Egyptian civilization lasted for 3000 years. Help the children create a giant timeline frieze for the classroom wall. See http://www.bbc.co.uk/history/ancient/egyptians/timeline.shtml

Useful websites
Try the Pyramid Challenge at http://www.bbc.co.uk/history/ancient/egyptians/launch_gms_pyramid_builder.shtml.

For Egyptian-style pictures using clip-art, try http://www.phillipmartin.info/clipart/egypt.htm

Visit this excellent primary school site at http://www.snaithprimary.eril.net/egindex.htm